Waltham Forest Libraries E

Please return this item by the last date stamped. The loan may be renewed unless required by another customer.

OCt 15		

Need to renew your books?
http://www.walthamforest.gov.uk/libraries or
Dial 0115 929 3388 for Callpoint – our 24/7 automated telephone renewal line. You will need your library card number and your PIN. If you do not know your PIN, contact your local library.

ANCIENT
GREECE

BY CHARLIE SAMUELS

FRANKLIN WATTS

LONDON•SYDNEY

First published in Great Britain in 2015 by
The Watts Publishing Group

Copyright © 2015 Brown Bear Books Ltd

All rights reserved.

For Brown Bear Books Ltd:
Editorial Director: Lindsey Lowe
Managing Editor: Tim Cooke
Children's Publisher: Anne O'Daly
Art Director: Jeni Child
Designer: Lynne Lennon
Picture Manager: Sophie Mortimer

Dewey no. 938

ISBN: 978 1 4451 4262 3

Printed in China

Franklin Watts
An imprint of
Hachette Children's Group
Part of the Watts Publishing Group
Carmelite House
50 Victoria Embankment
London EC4Y 0DZ

An Hachette UK company
www.hachette.co.uk

www.franklinwatts.co.uk

CONTENTS

INTRODUCTION	4
TECHNOLOGICAL BACKGROUND	6
AGRICULTURE	8
BUILDING	10
PARTHENON AND TEMPLES	12
SCULPTURE	14
THEATRES	16
SCIENCE AND KNOWLEDGE	18
ARCHIMEDES	20
ARISTOTLE	22
PYTHAGORAS	24
TRANSPORT	26
WARSHIPS	28
WEAPONS AND WARFARE	30
ASTRONOMY	32
MEASURING TIME	34
COINS AND METALS	36
MEDICINE	38
POTTERY	40
GLASS-MAKING	42
TIMELINE	44
GLOSSARY	46
FURTHER INFORMATION	47
INDEX	48

INTRODUCTION

The ancient Greeks lived around the Aegean Sea from about 1600 BCE until about 100 BCE, when their territory was absorbed into the Roman Empire. They were some of the most adventurous, creative and ingenious people who ever lived. On the Greek mainland, on the many islands, on the coast of what is now Turkey and in Greek colonies throughout the Mediterranean, ancient Greeks were among the most

The remarkable buildings of the Acropolis ('high city') in Athens were some of the architectural wonders of the ancient world.

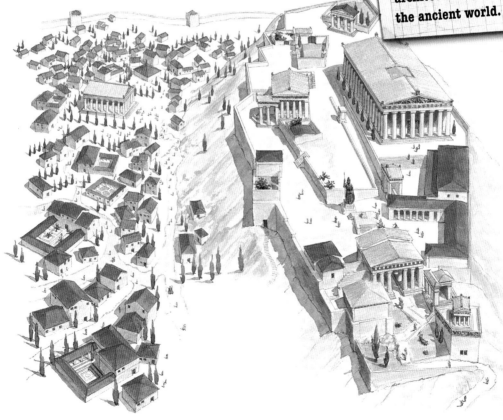

An advanced writing system allowed the Greeks to record the results of their studies, particularly of philosophy and maths.

inquisitive thinkers in history. While technology often improved in relatively small steps, Greek scientists tried to understand why things happened. They enjoyed learning as an intellectual challenge.

WARRING STATES

Ancient Greece was not united. It was a series of city-states, which frequently fought, but which all shared a similar culture and worshipped the same gods. The two most powerful city-states were Athens and Sparta. They were often at war, but sometimes made alliances to fight when threatened by others, such as Persia. This book will introduce you to the most important examples of the technology behind this remarkable period of intellectual development.

TECHNOLOGICAL BACKGROUND

The ancient Greeks emerged in a region that had been influenced by a number of earlier civilisations. The Greeks adopted the achievements of these other cultures. The ancient Egyptians had invented papyrus paper, which the Greeks used to write on. The Phoenician alphabet was the basis of Greek writing. The Greeks took the coinage invented in Lydia, in

The Greek alphabet was based on Phoenician writing, to which the Greeks added vowels.

modern-day Turkey, and improved it. They built magnificent temples and public buildings from marble, but their private homes were made from the same mud bricks as used by other cultures in the region. The Greeks used plumbing and understood the importance of clean water for health.

LOVE OF LEARNING

Unlike other peoples, however, the Greeks also enjoyed learning for its own sake. They created the first public library at Alexandria to share knowledge. Their idea of carefully observing the world was the foundation of modern medicine and astronomy. Their ways of thinking about the world's mysteries were the basis of modern philosophy.

The Minoans of Crete in the Greek Bronze Age had a complex system of plumbing to provide water for bathing.

AGRICULTURE

Farming was the basis of the ancient Greek economy. Eighty per cent of the population worked on the land. Farming was hard work. The soil was poor and the land was often hilly. The staple foods of the ancient Greeks were figs, grapes and olives. Such crops all needed plenty of sun but not much water.

A farmer uses oxen to plough a field while, in the background, workers harvest olives next to a field of grape-vines.

Olive trees grow easily in Greece, despite the poor soil, mountainous landscape and dry climate.

Greek farmers ploughed their fields twice a year: in spring and in the autumn. They made their ploughs from wood, and sometimes tipped them with iron. Farmers built flat terraces on the side of hills to increase the amount of land they could plant. They used irrigation and crop rotation to improve the poor soil.

FOOD SUPPLIES

Barley, a cereal, was the most important crop. It was grown between the rows of olive trees. Fish was also an important part of the diet. People caught fish on lines using bronze fish hooks. Wealthy people hunted wild deer, boar and hare using bows and arrows, nets and traps.

TECHNICAL SPECS

- Farmers harvested olives by beating the olive tree with whip-like branches until the fruit dropped to the ground.
- People used olive oil for cooking and eating, but also as a fuel for lamps and as a kind of soap.
- The Greeks made wine by treading on grapes. The wine was so thick it had to be strained using a bronze strainer. It was usually diluted with water.
- Raisins were made by letting grapes dry in the sunlight.
- Farmers kept goats to use for milk and cheese as well as for wool.
- Greece exported wine and olive oil. By producing a surplus, the ancient Greeks were able to become a powerful trading nation.

BUILDING

House at Olynthos

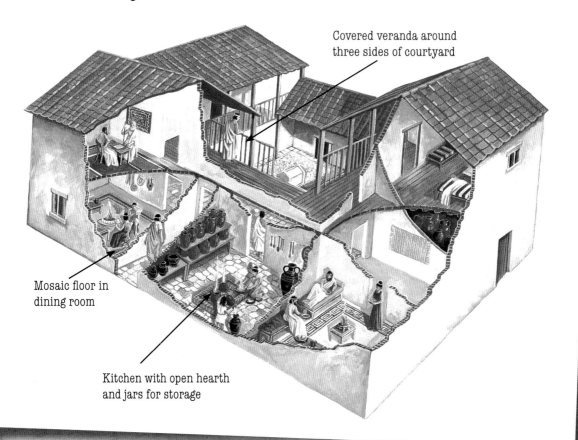

Covered veranda around three sides of courtyard

Mosaic floor in dining room

Kitchen with open hearth and jars for storage

There was a great difference between ancient Greek homes and public buildings. Little remains of domestic architecture, because people usually built houses from sun-dried mud bricks. For temples and the magnificent buildings of the cities, they used marble. Many buildings survive reasonably intact today.

The earliest type of ancient Greek house dates from around 1800 BCE. It had a main room or hall, called a *megaron*, with a hearth and columns to support the roof. From the fifth century BCE, the Greeks built houses around an open courtyard designed to keep the house cool in the hot summers. There was also a covered veranda along three sides of the courtyard to give shade.

FLOOR COVERINGS

Floors were finished with mosaic tiles in richer homes. In more modest homes, people probably plastered the bare earth or left it completely undecorated.

TECHNICAL SPECS

- Builders used wood only for doors, window shutters and roofs, because there was a shortage of suitable trees for building.
- The Greek city of Olynthos was destroyed on the orders of Philip of Macedonia in 348 BCE. Its ruins revealed the remains of ancient Greek homes.
- Houses in Olynthos were built in rows on a grid system.
- Women stayed out of sight. Their quarters were as far as possible from doors or windows that opened onto the street.
- Bricks for building houses were shaped from mud and left in the sun to dry.

Acropolis, Athens

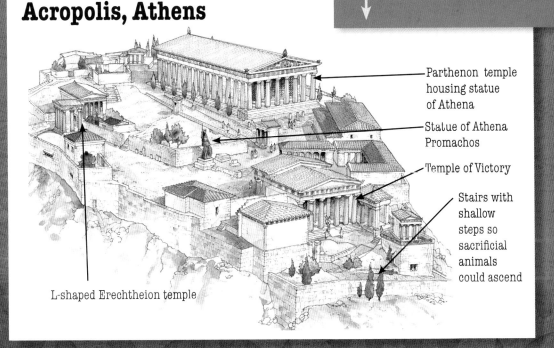

Parthenon temple housing statue of Athena

Statue of Athena Promachos

Temple of Victory

Stairs with shallow steps so sacrificial animals could ascend

L-shaped Erechtheion temple

PARTHENON AND TEMPLES

Ancient Greek architecture reached its peak in the temples. In Athens, the most magnificent buildings stood on the Acropolis (high city), a rocky hill overlooking the city. The most important building was the Parthenon built for the goddess Athena. It was a template (model) for public buildings.

The Parthenon

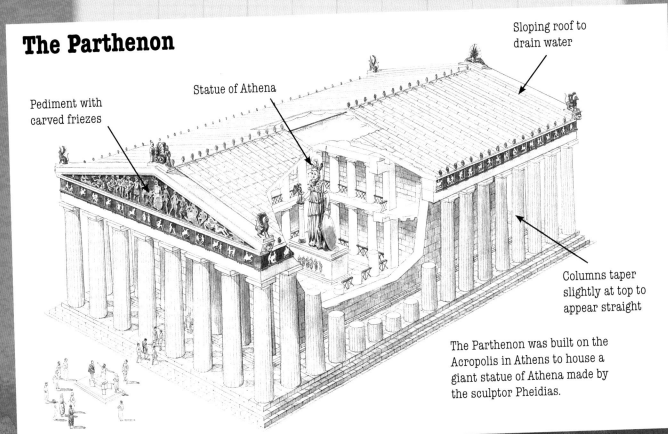

Sloping roof to drain water

Statue of Athena

Pediment with carved friezes

Columns taper slightly at top to appear straight

The Parthenon was built on the Acropolis in Athens to house a giant statue of Athena made by the sculptor Pheidias.

Columns were used to create porches outside Greek temples. There were three styles of column: Doric, Ionic and Corinthian.

Marble was plentiful in Greece. Masons quarried it by hammering wooden wedges into cracks in the rock, then soaking them with water. As the wet wood expanded, the marble cracked. The blocks were shaped in the quarry but were finely carved at the building site. They fitted together so well that no mortar was needed.

MAKING COLUMNS

Greek architecture is famous for its columns. Columns were made from squat, round cylinders of marble. To make a column, a number of these cylinders were pinned together using metal clips. The column was raised into place using ropes and pulleys.

TECHNICAL SPECS

- The Greeks used a form of skylight. They placed tiles of very thin marble in roofs to let light through.
- Doric columns were plain at the capital (top); Ionic columns had ram's-horn curls; Corinthian columns were decorated with carvings of acanthus leaves.
- The ancient Greeks used an optical illusion in the columns at the Parthenon. From a distance, straight columns look as though they bend outwards. To compensate for this, the Greeks made them taper slightly towards the top so that they appeared straight.
- Rainwater drained off temple roofs through spouts carved in the shape of animal heads.
- Decorative friezes were often added to the fronts of temples.

SCULPTURE

This marble statue of the god Apollo was carved early in the second century CE. It was a copy of a much earlier statue.

Sculptures were used in ancient Greece to decorate temples and other public buildings. The sculptors used limestone, marble or bronze. Sculpture could be statues or friezes, carved into the walls of buildings. There were three main subjects for the sculptures: battles, mythology and Greek rulers.

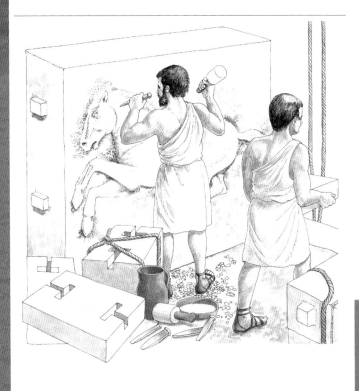

A worker carves a horse on a frieze. The blocks of marble were held together by pieces of metal inserted in the T-shaped holes.

The sculptor first created a full-size model from clay. The marble was chiselled into a rough form by copying the clay model before a master sculptor finished the carving. The surface was smoothed before the marble was painted.

BRONZE STATUES

Sculptors cast bronze statues using the 'lost-wax' method. They covered a wax model with clay, which was then baked. The wax melted and was poured out of the mould, which filled with molten metal that was left to harden. The clay was broken off to reveal the bronze statue.

TECHNICAL SPECS

- Friezes, such as the one on the Parthenon in Athens, were narrow bands of relief carvings that decorated the upper walls of temples.
- Friezes were painted bright colours.
- Statues were finished with metal attachments, such as spears, swords, bridles and other attachments such as women's jewellery.
- Bronze statues were finished using glass for eyes, copper for lips and silver for teeth and fingernails.
- Humans and gods were carved at the same size. Male statues were usually young and were often carved naked in order to show the Greek idea of the perfect human form.

THEATRES

Drama was one of the ancient Greeks' greatest innovations. The word 'drama' means 'action on stage'. Almost every Greek city had a theatre that put on dramas as part of religious festivals. The dramas were either tragedies or comedies.
In Athens, dramas in honour of Dionysus, the god of wine, resembled modern plays.

Behind the circular space where the chorus stood, the actors performed on a raised stage.

Actors used masks to impress or frighten the audience. Masks also allowed performers to play different characters.

Theatres were built on hillsides. They were shaped like horseshoes, with steps cut into the hillside to provide seating. The flat area at the bottom was called the orchestra.

ACOUSTIC ENGINEERING

A theatre could seat up to 18,000 people. The people at the back had to be able to hear the actors as well as the people in the front row could. The Greeks used maths to work out the best acoustics. In the theatre at Epidaurus, which is still used, speech from the stage is amplified by the bowl-like effect of the hillside.

TECHNICAL SPECS

- Actors entered the orchestra via a tall arched entrance called a *parodoi* or *eisodoi*.
- The seats in the front rows were wooden, so they could be removed; the rest were stone. The best seats at the front were reserved for officials, visitors and competition judges.
- Stone tokens were used as tickets. They were marked with seat numbers.
- Special effects included a *mechane* (crane) that made it look as though an actor was flying, and trapdoors in the floor used to bring actors on stage.
- From 465 BCE, a scenic wall was hung or stood behind the orchestra. Death scenes always took place behind this *skene* (from which the modern word 'scene' comes).

SCIENCE AND KNOWLEDGE

The *School of Athens*, painted by Raphael in 1510, shows famous Greek philosophers, with Plato and Aristotle in the centre.

The ancient Greeks were the first people to separate philosophy – the study of ideas – from science. Around the sixth century BCE, the Greeks began carefully observing the world. This taught them, for example, that sickness is often caused by bad hygiene, not by the gods, as had been thought. Observations made the Greeks rethink how they looked at the world.

Although the Greeks attempted to understand more about the world, they did not write down many of their discoveries. As a result, historians once believed that the ancient Greeks had not been interested in science.

GREEK INVENTIONS

Today we know this belief was wrong. For example, the Greeks developed the world's first computer. The so-called Antikythera mechanism was probably used to calculate the movements of the Sun and Moon. Other Greek inventions included the steam engine and the slot machine.

The Greeks loved all types of knowledge. They opened the first public library in the third century BCE. It was in the Museum of Alexandria, in Egypt, which was an early research institute.

TECHNICAL SPECS

- The Antikythera mechanism was found in 1900 in an ancient shipwreck. It took scientists a century to realise that it was a computer made up of a series of different-sized wheels.
- Heron of Alexandria invented the world's first slot machine. It was used at temples to dispense holy water for washing as a person entered the temple.
- Heron also invented the first simple steam engine. A pot filled with water was placed over a fire. Two tubes carried steam into a hollow metal ball, where it flowed out through two more angled tubes. The expelled steam made the ball rotate.

This steam engine was invented by Heron. Steam expelled from the bent tubes made the ball rotate.

ARCHIMEDES

One of the greatest mathematicians who ever lived, Archimedes was also a prolific inventor. Some of his inventions are still in use today. Schoolchildren use one of Archimedes' inventions daily without realising it: he calculated the value of pi in order to work out the area of a circle.

One of the weapons Archimedes is said to have built to defend Syracuse was a lens that focused the Sun's rays to set fire to enemy ships.

HOW TO...

The Archimedes screw pump was a spiral screw inside a cylinder. As the screw was turned, it raised the water from one level to another by pushing it against the side of the cylinder. The ancient Egyptians used the screw to raise water from the Nile to irrigate crops. The screw is still used in many parts of the world today.

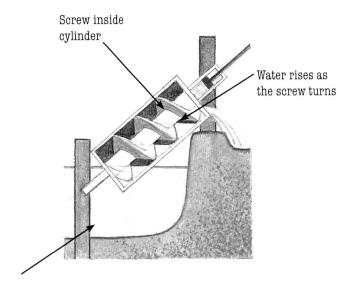

Screw inside cylinder

Water rises as the screw turns

Supply of water

Archimedes was not the first person to use levers, but he was the first person to understand the principle behind them. He calculated the length of lever needed to move any object. He used a lever to single-handedly lift a ship out of a dry dock and into the sea.

WEAPONS TECHNOLOGY

Archimedes invented weapons to protect his city of Syracuse from a Roman attack. He rebuilt the city walls to accommodate cranes that dropped boulders onto the enemy. It was said that another weapon, the 'claw', lifted enemy ships up and overturned them.

TECHNICAL SPECS

- Archimedes' claw was probably a crane with a grappling hook.
- Archimedes is said to have invented the first fire engine, a cart that carried water.
- Archimedes discovered the principle of the displacement of water when he got into a full bath and it overflowed.
- King Hieron was worried that his gold crown had been mixed with silver. Silver weighs less than gold. Archimedes measured the water displaced by the crown against the water displaced by a solid gold object of the same weight. He proved that the king's crown was not solid gold.

ARISTOTLE

Deliquiũ Solis poſt natũ Chriſtum
Anno 15 44 die 24 Ianuarii

This 17th-century diagram shows the principle of Aristotle's camera obscura, which projected an upside-down image onto a wall.

Aristotle was probably the most influential thinker who has ever lived. His work covered every subject of study known in ancient Greece, including politics, logic, meteorology, physics and theology. He still influences modern thought. The camera obscura he invented is still used today.

Aristotle tried to separate philosophy from science. He was the first person to spell out that science is based on careful observation. Aristotle proved that the Earth is round by observing the curved shadow it cast on the Moon during a lunar eclipse.

DEFINING SCIENCE

Aristotle estimated the diameter of the Earth to within 50 per cent of its true value. He observed that, as he travelled north or south, new stars appeared on one horizon while others fell below the other horizon. This happened after even a short distance, showing clearly that the Earth was not flat.

Aristotle was a founder of Western philosophy. He studied with Plato and was the tutor of the young Alexander the Great.

TECHNICAL SPECS

- Aristotle believed that matter was composed of four elements: earth, air, water and fire. The heavens were made of a fifth, 'aether'.
- Aristotle believed that the heavens were unchanging and perfect, while Earth was changeable.
- Aristotle's careful observation set the standard for future scientific study. He was one of the first to collect plant specimens and classify them into groups.
- The camera obscura was the forerunner of the camera. It was a dark box with a small hole in one side. Light passing through the hole formed an inverted image on the opposite side of the box. The device allowed people to observe eclipses safely.

PYTHAGORAS

Pythagoras was a Greek mathematician, astronomer and philosopher. He is most famous for the Pythagorean theorem, which is still used in classrooms to help to calculate areas.

Pythagoras had many followers. They settled in a Greek colony in southern Italy. Pythagoras greatly influenced the younger Greek philosopher Plato. In turn, Plato influenced generations of later philosophers.

In this medieval drawing, Pythagoras tests the sounds produced by different sizes of bell, or glasses containing different amounts of liquid.

Pythagoras's followers were known as the Pythagoreans. They believed that the Earth was a sphere at the centre of a spherical universe. They believed that the planets occupied their own transparent spheres. These spheres were spaced out evenly and rotated around Earth.

MATHS IN EVERYTHING

Pythagoras believed the whole world could be seen through maths. He saw a particularly close link between music and maths. He discovered that the intervals between musical notes could be expressed in mathematical terms. Apart from his theorem, Pythagoras's main contribution to science was the realisation that answers to scientific problems usually led to new problems.

TECHNICAL SPECS

- Pythagoras's theorem is about the shape and area of right-angled triangles. The theory had been known to the Sumerians and to the ancient Chinese, but the Greek thinker proved it was right.
- Pythagoras described square numbers, cube numbers and spherical numbers before they were fully understood.
- The Pythagoreans treated men and women equally, which was unknown in ancient Greece.
- Pythagoras left no original writings, so everything we know about him comes from his followers and his critics.

$$a^2 + b^2 = c^2$$

Pythagoras's theorem says that the area of the square of the longest side of a triangle equals the squares of the two other sides.

TRANSPORT

The Greek mainland and islands are surrounded by water. The terrain is mountainous and the ancient Greeks had few roads. They travelled mainly by ship. When they travelled on land, it was usually on foot. The thinker Socrates once walked from Athens to Olympia, a total of 330 kilometres (200 miles), in five or six days.

Cargo ship

Ancient Greece relied on shipping, both to communicate with the many islands and to carry trade goods and settlers throughout the Mediterranean. Earlier vessels had a curved prow (front) and one row of oars.

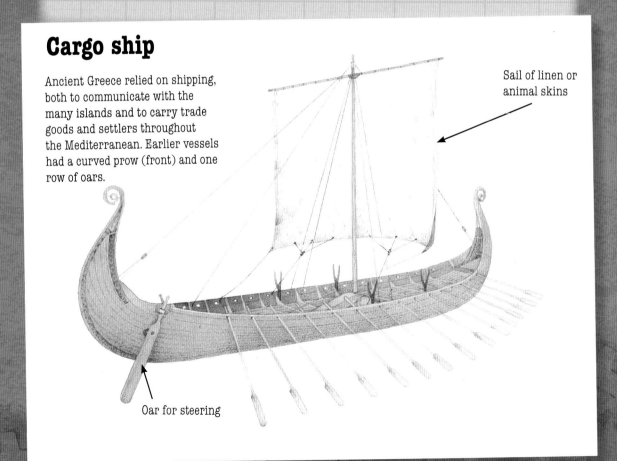

Sail of linen or animal skins

Oar for steering

Pharos at Alexandria

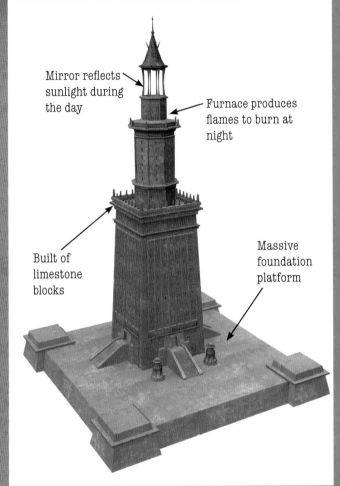

Mirror reflects sunlight during the day

Furnace produces flames to burn at night

Built of limestone blocks

Massive foundation platform

TECHNICAL SPECS

- Sea travel was dangerous because of pirates, bad weather and poor navigation. The Greeks built the world's first lighthouse (Pharos) at Alexandria to guide ships safely into the harbour.

- The Dioklos was a paved road of limestone blocks. Two parallel grooves 1.5 metres (5 feet) apart held the wheels of trolleys pushed by slaves.

- The ancient Greeks improved Babylonian maps. They invented both latitude and longitude and the major lines of latitude, such as the Equator, the Tropic of Cancer and the Tropic of Capricorn.

LAND TRANSPORT

A cart track allowed goods to be carried the 8 kilometres (5 miles) between the port of Piraeus and Athens. For short journeys, people used chariots; for longer distances, some people went by mule. The Greeks rarely rode horses: they had no saddles, stirrups or horseshoes. The Greeks built a paved trackway, Dioklos, that ran 6.5 kilometres (4 miles) across the Isthmus of Corinth. The Dioklos was a major engineering achievement. It meant small warships or empty cargo vessels could be pulled across the isthmus rather than having to sail around the peninsula.

WARSHIPS

A trireme rams an enemy vessel. Triremes had a few armed soldiers on deck ready to board a rammed ship.

Athens, the most powerful of the Greek city-states, controlled its empire by means of its navy. The Athenians called their navy their 'wooden walls'. By controlling the Aegean Sea, the Athenians could decide which goods and which troops went to and from the islands. The warships also protected Athens' merchant vessels from attack as they brought food and luxuries to the port of Piraeus.

TECHNICAL SPECS

- The name 'trireme' comes from the ships' three banks of oars.
- Triremes dominated the eastern Mediterranean between the seventh and fourth centuries BCE.
- A drummer sometimes played a beat on the trireme to keep the rowers in time.
- Boatbuilders used four main types of wood to make ships: fir, pine, cedar and oak. They mainly used oak for the hulls. The ships had to be light enough to be carried up onto the beach.
- In favourable sailing conditions, a trireme could cover up to 95 kilometres (60 miles) in a day.

The ancient Greeks had one type of warship: the trireme. Power for this wooden galley (rowed ship) came from up to 170 oarsmen sitting in three rows. At its most powerful, the city-state of Athens had 300 triremes in service.

RAMMING TACTICS

At its bow (front), below the waterline, the trireme had a wooden ram covered in bronze. To sink an enemy ship, the trireme would ram it in the side. If the enemy boat did not sink, soldiers boarded it. Crews spent long periods practising ramming and boarding manoeuvres.

Trireme cross section

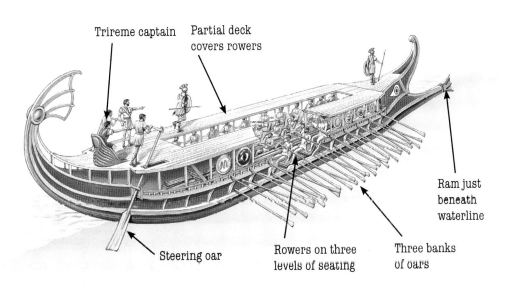

Trireme captain

Partial deck covers rowers

Ram just beneath waterline

Steering oar

Rowers on three levels of seating

Three banks of oars

WEAPONS AND WARFARE

The ancient Greek city-states often fought each other. Many Greek men joined an army. In Athens, boys trained as soldiers between the ages of 18 and 20 and could be called up for military service. In Sparta, the organisation of the whole state was based on warfare. Warriors called hoplites controlled the land; the trireme controlled the seas.

Hoplites fought in close formations known as *phalanxes*. Their shields overlapped to form a wall.

Spartan hoplites prepare to raid enemy territory. Sparta was the most warlike of the city-states.

Between the seventh and fourth centuries BCE, the hoplite dominated warfare. Hoplites came from wealthy families, who paid for their armour and weapons. Poorer soldiers often served as archers and stone-slingers.

SIEGE WARFARE

Sieges were an important part of warfare. Armies used catapults, fire and stone-slingers to attack a walled city. The defenders dropped burning coals and sulphur on the attackers.

TECHNICAL SPECS

- The breastplate consisted of two metal plates joined at the sides by leather straps. The sides of the upper body were left exposed.
- Helmets were vital, because when hoplites marched in a phalanx, their heads were left exposed.
- Military commanders were called *strategoi*, the source of the English word 'strategy'.
- Cavalrymen would not willingly charge a phalanx as they and the horses risked being speared.
- Phalanxes tried to break a gap in the opposing phalanx to attack the enemy's flanks and rear.
- Shields were held by a strap that went around the hoplite's arm. There was also a handle to grip.

ASTRONOMY

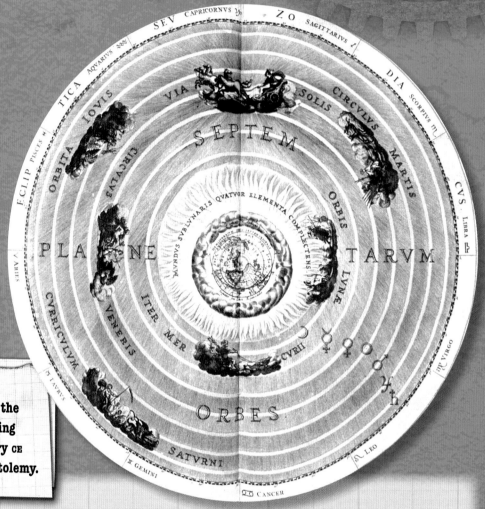

This diagram shows the solar system according to the second-century CE Greek astronomer Ptolemy.

The ancient Greeks contributed enormously to our understanding of astronomy, the study of heavenly bodies. They were the first people to realise the Earth was round and that the Moon reflected the light of the Sun. They also suggested that the Earth was not fixed but moved around the Sun.

When the ancient Greek scientist and natural philosopher Thales of Miletus (c.624–545 BCE) visited Egypt in 600 BCE, he returned with a knowledge of Babylonian astronomy and maths. Introducing maths to the study of the planets and stars was a huge breakthrough in astronomy.

UNDERSTANDING THE SKIES

Early Greeks had seen the heavenly bodies as gods that controlled their lives. Anaxagoras (c.500–428 BCE) was the first person to suggest that the Sun was not a god but a burning mass of metal. Once the Greeks stopped seeing heavenly bodies as gods, they started to calculate the movements of the planets and stars. This allowed them to predict the changing seasons, which was vital help for sailors and farmers.

TECHNICAL SPECS

- The Greeks understood orbits. Each month the Moon seemed to shrink and grow. The Greeks reasoned that something passing in front changed its appearance.
- Astronomers knew about the planets Mercury, Venus, Mars, Jupiter and Saturn.
- Aristarchus of Samos (third century BCE) suggested that the Earth rotates on its axis and the Sun is stationary, both of which were proved true centuries later.
- Eratosthenes of Cyrene (third century BCE) worked out the circumference of Earth as 47,000 kilometres (29,206 miles). The correct figure is actually 40,075 kilometres (24,902 miles).

A medieval illustration shows the goddess of astronomy instructing Ptolemy about the heavens.

MEASURING TIME

Discovered in an ancient shipwreck, the Antikythera mechanism was made about 100 BCE to calculate the movement of heavenly bodies.

The ancient Greeks needed to record the changing seasons so they knew when to plant and harvest their crops. In the ninth century BCE, the poet Hesiod noted that the cry of migrating cranes was the sign that it was time for farmers to plough and sow. Beyond that, each city-state followed its own calendar.

MEASURING TIME

The first water clocks were pottery jars with holes for water to drip through. A large public water clock in Athens, however, had a marker on the outside to show the time. Later clocks were more intricate. Andronichos designed the 'tower of the winds' in the first century BCE. It was a complicated water clock that gave the time on the sundial on top of the tower, while a rotating disc showed the movements of the stars and the course of the Sun through the constellations.

Advanced water clock

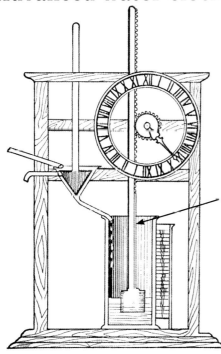

Water supply drips into tank, raising the float

In this water clock, a float rising in the main tank of water raises a toothed rod, which turns a toothed cog to rotate the hand on a clock face, indicating the passage of time.

TECHNICAL SPECS

- A Greek day lasted from sunset to sunset (not midnight to midnight like the modern day).
- Like other ancient cultures, the Greeks counted 12 hours of daytime and 12 of night.
- The Greeks divided their year into 12 months, with a 13th month added to balance the cycle every eight years from the fifth to the middle of the fourth century BCE.
- Different states started their years at different times. The Athenians kept three calendars. One was for religious festivals. The second was political. The third was astronomical.
- A water clock invented by Ctesibius of Alexandria in 270 BCE used valves to operate ringing bells, moving puppets and singing birds.

COINS AND METALS

The early ancient Greeks bartered for goods, but by 600 BCE, trade was flourishing and payment in coins became common. The first coins were lumps of precious metal, which was found in numerous parts of Greece. The silver mine at Laurium made Athens wealthy.

The tunnels in Greek mines could be as deep as 100 metres (330 feet) and working conditions were harsh. Slaves worked in the mines, using picks and iron hammers to extract the ore.

This silver coin was minted in Athens in the fifth century BCE. It features an owl, the symbol of Athena, goddess of wisdom.

TECHNICAL SPECS

- Coinage was introduced into Greece from Lydia in Asia Minor (modern-day Turkey).
- In ancient Athens, a skilled worker earned one silver *drachma* per day; one-sixth of a drachma was an *obol*.
- People only used gold coins after the fourth century BCE. Less valuable bronze coins appeared at the end of the fifth century BCE.
- Since coinage was a mark of independence, every city had its own mint.
- Greek mines included not just the silver mine at Laurium, but also iron, gold and copper mines.

Bronze was used for weapons and armour. In the fifth century BCE, the Athenians tipped their swords with even harder steel.

The first coins in Greece were made from electrum, an alloy of gold and silver. From the sixth century BCE, the usual metal for coins was pure silver. Each city-state had its own coinage.

Athenian silver coins were stamped with an owl. It was the symbol of wisdom and of Athena, the goddess of the city.

EARLY COINAGE

As the number of coins in circulation increased, industries developed that were based on money. Money exchange and banking became common professions in the late fifth century BCE.

MEDICINE

The ancient Greeks took a huge step forward in medicine. Although they believed that sickness could be caused by the gods, they realised that good health was also a result of a person's behaviour, environment and diet. To reflect this, ancient Greek medicine combined two types of treatment. One was based on magic and the other on examining a patient and keeping him or her healthy.

The Greek god of medicine and healing was Asclepius, a son of the god Apollo. Healing took place in his temples. Greeks went to sleep there when they were ill, or left gifts for the gods.

The ruins of the Asclepion still stand at Epidaurus. Snakes were sacred, so they were allowed to crawl around the temple.

A doctor examines a patient with an injured arm. Greek doctors could set broken limbs, but they avoided surgery if they could.

The Greeks believed Asclepius appeared in a 'magical dream' in which he prescribed treatments such as herbal remedies, diets and exercise. The following day, priests at the temple would administer these cures.

HIPPOCRATES

The cult of Asclepius led to the development of medical treatments for all kinds of diseases. The greatest advances came in the Hellenistic period (323–30 BCE). But the most influential doctor was Hippocrates (c.460–c.370 BCE). He was the first to describe many diseases, such as the clubbing of fingers (when fingers become thick, a sign of lung disease).

TECHNICAL SPECS

- In 400 BCE, Hippocrates wrote down rules about how a doctor should treat a patient. Many doctors still swear the Hippocratic Oath when they learn medicine.
- Doctors tried to avoid surgery, because they saw that patients became ill after surgery from shock, loss of blood or infections.
- The Greeks were the first people to make sure that all their cities had public fountains to supply clean water to maintain health.
- The first medical school opened at Cnidus around 700 BCE. Students there learned to observe their patients' symptoms.
- Alcmaeon, who wrote the first study of human anatomy between about 500 and 450 BCE, worked at the medical school at Cnidus.

POTTERY

Ancient Greek pottery is one of the best sources of information about daily life two-and-a-half thousand years ago. The Greeks decorated pottery with many different scenes, and while few Greek paintings and little writing have survived, many pots and pottery fragments have.

An Athenian potter shapes a vase on a wheel. Pottery was normally made and painted by different people, like a modern-day production line.

The earliest ancient Greek pots were decorated with geometric patterns. In the seventh century BCE, potters in Corinth began making pots with black figures cut into the clay.

POTTERY PEAK

The peak of ancient Greek pottery was the Athenian period from the sixth to fourth centuries BCE. In the black-figure technique, artists painted figures on pots in special slip (wet clay) that turned black during firing (heating). Around 530 BCE, the red-figure technique was introduced. Now the pot was black but areas that were not painted with slip showed through as red figures.

It was easier to show detail in the red-figure technique, because the black-figure technique only allowed the creation of silhouettes.

TECHNICAL SPECS

- Larger pots were made in stages on a potter's wheel. Potters threw the neck and body separately and joined them together. They later attached the feet and handles.
- Ancient Greek pots were fired in three stages. In the first stage, the potter let air into the kiln. This turned the whole vase the colour of the red clay. In the next stage, the potter burned green wood to reduce the oxygen supply. The pot turned black in the smoke. In the final stage, the potter reintroduced air to the kiln; unpainted areas turned back to red, while the painted areas remained black.
- There were specific vessels for carrying food and wine (*amphora*), drawing water (*hydria*), and for drinking water and wine (*kantharos* or *kylix*).
- Potters created the metallic glaze of the black slip by using special clay collected from local clay beds.

GLASS-MAKING

These glass vessels were made in Greece during the Roman period, in about the fifth century CE.

Like the ancient Egyptians and Romans, the ancient Greeks prized glassware. They did not know about glass-blowing until late in their history. Instead, the Greeks produced their glassware using first the core method and then a method known as slumping. As glass-makers became more skilled, they were able to produce larger objects.

The Mesopotamians first made glass around 3500 BCE from a mixture of quartz sand (silica), soda and lime. Like them, the early Greeks made glassware using the core method. The hot glass mixture was poured over a core made from clay. Once the glass had cooled, the core was removed.

COLOURED GLASS

Later, the Greeks poured viscous glass into moulds to make shapes. To make multicoloured glass, threads of glass coloured by adding oxides were shaped around the mould. This method was used to make dishes and beads, and for containers such as amphorae.

TECHNICAL SPECS

- Glass was almost as precious as gold in ancient Greece.
- There were three terms for glass: 'kyanos' referred to dark blue, shiny material, 'lithos chyte' meant molten stone and 'hyalos' was everyday glass.
- The ancient Mycenaeans used glass, but no workshops have so far been discovered in Mycenae.
- Historians think that there was a large glass-making workshop on the island of Rhodes.
- Glass-makers cast glass to be used for mosaics in a flat, open mould and then cut it into pieces.
- During the Hellenistic period, thin layers of gold were put between layers of transparent glass. Craftworkers also made cameo, a kind of light-coloured glass on a dark glass background.

This fourth-century CE glass vial has two handles so it can be lifted to the mouth for drinking.

TIMELINE

BCE	
c.1100	The Dark Ages begin in Greece as the Mycenacan civilisation declines and the Dorians and Ionians invade.
c.800	The Greeks develop vowels to use with consonants taken from the Phoenician alphabet.
776	The first Olympic Games are held.
c.700	Gold coins are used as money in Lydia in western Anatolia (Turkey).
c.700	Glaucus of Chios is said to learn how to solder iron together.
c.650	The trireme replaces the bireme as the standard Greek warship.
c.600	Thales of Miletus introduces Babylonian mathematics to Greece.
c.600	Sundials are used to measure time.
c.600	Theodorus of Samos is said to invent smelting ores and casting metals.
c.600	Alcmaeon writes the first book on human anatomy (body structure).
c.585	Thales of Miletus predicts a solar eclipse.
c.530	Among other discoveries, Pythagoras proposes that musical intervals are based on mathematics, and that sound is a vibration in the air.
c.479	Athens enters a golden age that lasts until 431 BCE.
c.450	Anaxagoras of Athens explains eclipses by proposing that the Moon reflects sunlight and has no illumination of its own.
c.440	The 'lost-wax' process is used for casting objects in bronze.
c.440	Hippocrates argues that diseases have natural rather than supernatural causes.

c.425	The Thebans are said to use a flamethrower in an attack on Delium.
399	Engineers at Syracuse invent an arrow-firing catapult to defend the city.
387	Plato founds his academy in Athens.
c.375	Archytas of Tarentum builds the first automaton (robot) and studies mechanics.
c.340	Praxagoras of Crete discovers the difference between veins and arteries.
c.335	Aristotle founds the Lyceum in Athens.
c.330	Aristotle uses the camera obscura to study projection.
327	Alexander the Great of Macedon begins his campaigns of conquest.
c.300	Euclid writes *Elements*, for centuries a standard work on geometry.
c.280	The Pharos of Alexandria is built; it is the world's first lighthouse.
c.270	Ctesibius of Alexandria invents a water clock that uses mechanical gears.
c.245	The library of Alexandria is catalogued for the first time.
c.240	Eratosthenes of Cyrene calculates the diameter of the Earth.
c.225	Archimedes invents the Archimedes screw.
c.170	Parchment is invented in Pergamon; it replaces papyrus as writing material.
c.134	Hipparchus measures the year more accurately than anyone before him.
CE	
45	Sosigenes of Alexandria devises a calendar of 365.25 days, adopted by the Roman emperor Julius Caesar (the Julian calendar).
60	Heron of Alexandria builds the first steam engine, and describes many automata (robots).

GLOSSARY

acoustics The science of sound.

acropolis Greek for 'high city';
a fortified part of a city on a height.

barter To trade by swapping goods for
other goods.

city-state A city that governs itself and the
surrounding territory.

crop rotation Varying the crops grown in
fields to give the soil a chance to recover.

displacement The action by which an object
put into water moves away an equal volume
of water.

eclipse When one heavenly body passes in
front of another.

frieze In architecture, a band of
carved decoration, often around the top
of a building.

geometric Describes a pattern of regular lines
and shapes.

glaze A thin, glass-like layer applied to the
surface of pottery.

hearth A fireplace and its surroundings.

Hellenistic Related to classical Greece.

Hellenistic period The late period of ancient
Greece, from 323 BCE to the first century CE.

helmsman The person in charge of steering a
ship.

hoplite A Greek infantry soldier.

hull The main body of a ship, including the
bottom, sides and deck.

irrigation Artificially watering the land to
grow crops.

lime A white substance that is extracted
from limestone.

mosaic A decoration made by using small
pieces of coloured glass or ceramic to cover
a surface.

Mycenaeans The inhabitants of Mycenae,
an important city-state during the Greek
bronze age.

orchestra A semicircular space for
performances in a Greek theatre.

ore Rocks and minerals in which metals
naturally occur.

oxide A mineral that includes oxygen.

phalanx A formation in which soldiers
formed lines with overlapping shields.

philosophy An attempt to understand
reality by observation, logical thought
and deduction.

slip A mixture of clay and water used for
decorating pots.

smelting Extracting metal from an ore by
using heat.

soda A mineral also known as sodium
carbonate.

staple A food that makes up the major part
of a diet.

template Something that serves as a model
and can be reproduced.

theorem A mathematical proposal that can
be shown to be true.

trireme A rowed warship with three banks of
oars.

veranda A roofed platform along the outside
of a house

vial A small lidded container for holding
liquid medicines.

viscous Having a thick, sticky consistency
between solid and liquid.

FURTHER INFORMATION

BOOKS

Ancient Greece (Eyewitness). Dorling Kindersley, 2014.

Ancient Greece (Facts at Your Fingertips). Wayland, 2009.

Deary, Terry. *The Groovy Greeks* (Horrible Histories). Scholastic, 2007.

Freeman, Maggie. *Great Archimedes* (Spotlight on Fact). Collins Educational, 2002.

MacDonald, Fiona. *Ancient Greece (100 Facts)*. Miles Kelly Publishing, 2009.

Minay, Rachel. *Ancient Greece* (The History Detective Investigates). Wayland, 2015.

Parker, Steve. *Aristotle* (Great Scientists). Belitha Press, 2003.

Sims, Lesley. *A Visitor's Guide to Ancient Greece* (Usborne Visitor Guides). Usborne Publishing, 2014.

WEBSITES

www.britishmuseum.org/explore/young_explorers/discover/museum_explorer/ancient_greece/tools_and_technology.aspx/
British Museum guide to tools and technology in ancient Greece.

www.primaryresources.co.uk/history/history5b.htm
Primarysources.com page with links to ancient Greek subjects.

www.swan.ac.uk/grst/Home Page G&RS&T.htm
Pages hosted by Swansea University about technology in ancient Greece and Rome.

Note to parents and teachers: In the book every effort has been made by the Publishers to ensure that websites are suitable for children, that they are of the highest educational value, and that they contain no inappropriate or offensive material. However, because of the nature of the Internet, it is impossible to guarantee that the contents of these sites will not be altered. We advise that Internet access is supervised by a responsible adult.

INDEX

acoustic engineering 17
Acropolis 11
actors 17
agriculture 8-9
alphabet, Greek 6
alphabet, Phoenician 6
Anaxagoras 33
Antikythera mechanism 19, 34
Archimedes 20–21
Archimedes' claw 21
Archimedes' screw 21
Aristotle 22–23
astronomy 7, 32–33

bricks 7, 10
building 10–11

calendars 35
camera obscura 22, 23
chariots 27
city-states 28, 34
Cnidus, medical school 39
coins 6, 36–37
columns 13
core method 41–42

Dioklos trackway 27

eclipse, lunar 23
Egyptians 6
electrum 37
Epidaurus 38

friezes 13, 14, 15

glass 42–43
glass-blowing 42

Heron of Alexander 19, 45
Hippocrates 39, 44
hoplites 30–31

inventions 19
irrigation 9

kiln 41
knowledge 18–19

Larium silver mine 36, 37
lighthouse 27

marble 15
mask 17
medicine 7, 38–39
Mesopotamians 42
metals 36–37
mosaics 42

olives 8–9
Olynthos 11
oxen 8

papyrus 6
Parthenon 12–13
philosophy 18, 23
Plato 24
ploughs 9
plumbing 7
pottery 40–41
priests 39
Ptolemy 33
Pythagoras 24–25
Pythagoras's theorem 24, 25

science 18–19, 23, 25

sculpture 14–15
ships 26
siege warfare 31
slaves 36
Socrates 26
soldiers 30
statues 15
steam engine 19

temples 7, 10, 12–13, 38–39
theatres 16–17
time, measuring 34–35
trade 36
transportation 26–27
trireme 28, 29, 30

vases 41

warfare 30–31
warships 28–29
water clocks 35
water, displacement 21
weapons 30–31
wheel, potter's 41